THE DRED SCOTT DECISION

DRED SCOTT, a slave from the slave state of Missouri, had been taken by his master to the free state of Illinois and then to a free territory. Back in Missouri, Scott sued for his freedom on the grounds that he had lived in both a free state and territory. But the Supreme Court, headed by Roger Taney, ruled that he was not a U.S. citizen and therefore could not sue anybody in a court of law; that he was his master's personal property; and that as a resident of Missouri he could not be bound by Illinois law. The Court also said Scott could not be freed because Congress had no right to take away personal property without due process of law. This last ruling declared the Missouri Compromise to be unconstitutional since it barred slavery north of the 36° 30′ line. The historic verdict further inflamed the controversy between North and South.

PRINCIPALS

DRED SCOTT, Negro slave owned by Peter Blow.

ROGER B. TANEY, Chief Justice of the U.S. Supreme Court, who ruled against Dred Scott's suit for freedom.

PETER BLOW, original owner of Dred Scott.

DR. JOHN EMERSON, Army surgeon to whom Peter Blow's daughter sold Scott.

MRS. IRENE SANFORD EMERSON, widow of Dr. Emerson, who left Scott with Henry Blow when she moved to New York.

HENRY BLOW, son of Peter Blow, who financed Scott's first suit for freedom.

DR. CALVIN C. CHAFFEE, Mrs. Emerson's second husband, sought a Supreme Court decision on Scott's rights.

JOHN F. A. SANFORD, Mrs. Emerson's brother, to whom Scott was "sold" before Scott's lawyers started his suit for freedom.

PRESIDENT JAMES BUCHANAN, who wrote an unusual and not exactly proper letter to Supreme Court Justice John Catron.

Dred Scott couldn't understand "all the fuss they made in Washington." But the "fuss" over him drastically changed the lives of many important men. The man whom Scott's case helped the most was Abraham Lincoln. (Culver Pictures)

A FOCUS BOOK

The Dred Scott Decision
March 6, 1857

Slavery and the Supreme Court's "Self-Inflicted Wound"

by Frank B. Latham

Illustrated with contemporary prints

FRANKLIN WATTS, INC.

575 Lexington Avenue   New York, N.Y. 10022

For Lucille and Linda

The authors and publishers of The Focus Books wish to acknowledge the helpful editorial suggestions of Professor Richard B. Morris.

2 3 4 5

Contents

THE DRED SCOTT DECISION

The Taney Decision on Dred Scott, March 6, 1857

On March 6, 1857, a tense, hushed crowd gathered in the Supreme Court room in the north wing of the Capitol Building in Washington, D.C. The Court crier banged his gavel and announced: "Oyez! Oyez! Oyez! All persons having business before the Honorable Supreme Court of the United States are admonished to draw near and give their attention, for the Court is now sitting. God save the United States and this Honorable Court."

Chief Justice Roger Brooke Taney, his face seamed by the wrinkles of his eighty years, then read the majority opinion of the Court in the case of *Dred Scott v. Sandford*. The frail Chief Justice declared that a Negro slave, or a free Negro whose ancestors were slaves, could not be a United States citizen, and that Congress had no power to keep slavery out of the territories of the United States.

Taney believed that the Court's decision would settle once and for all the question of slavery in the territories. Seldom in history has a man made a more dangerous miscalculation. For twenty-five years, the rights and wrongs of slavery had been debated both in and out of Congress with steadily growing bitterness. Instead of settling the question, the Supreme Court's decision on Dred Scott so aroused people that slavery's fate could be settled only by war. If war was not unavoidable, the decision made it so. How did this highly significant decision come about?

Who Was Dred Scott?

Dred Scott himself took little interest in the case that would help plunge the nation into disunion and Civil War in 1861. A skinny, sickly man who could neither read nor write, Dred was puzzled by "all the fuss they made in Washington." Scott had been born in Southampton County, Virginia, around the year 1795. His original owner, Peter Blow, moved his family and slaves to St. Louis, Missouri, in 1827 when Scott was about thirty-two. During that year, there were rumors of slave unrest throughout the South. Jumpy plantation owners recalled an earlier slave revolt led by a man named Denmark Vesey in 1822. They and their overseers carried shotguns as they made their rounds. Heavily armed patrols watched the roads at night. The slave code of the South decreed that slaves were not men. No promise made to a slave by his master need be kept. A slave or his children could be sold like a horse or cow. He could not own or sell anything. He could not testify in court or sue his master, and he might be condemned to death merely for striking a white person.

This time of tension and scare talk may have caused Peter Blow to move west. At any rate, if he had not moved, there might have been no Dred Scott case. On August 21, 1831, Southampton County was swept by a slave revolt. It was led by a Negro named Nat Turner, who believed God had chosen him to free his people from bondage. Turner's master had been kind to him. But when the killing began, this planter and his family were butchered with axes. Peter Blow and his family could easily have suffered the same fate.

Sixty whites and more than one hundred Negroes were killed before the Turner revolt was crushed. Subsequently, thirteen more slaves and three free Negroes were tried and hanged. Turner was finally run down and executed on November 11, 1831. "I am here," he said calmly, "loaded with chains, and willing to suffer the fate that awaits me."

Virginia and other southern states quickly passed harsher laws to control Negroes. Since Turner had been able to read and write, a law was passed forbidding anyone to educate a slave. The South now bristled with armed men, who kept a wary eye on several million slaves.

Dred's first master, Peter Blow, died in St. Louis in 1831, and Scott became the property of Blow's daughter Elizabeth. Two years

In 1836, Scott's master, Dr. John Emerson, bought a slave woman named Harriet from a Major Taliaferro, at Fort Snelling, Wisconsin Territory. That same year, Scott obtained permission from Dr. Emerson to marry Harriet, and the couple had a child they named Eliza. They had another child after they were taken back to Missouri by Dr. Emerson. (Culver Pictures)

later, she sold Scott to an Army surgeon, Dr. John Emerson. In 1834, the War Department transferred Dr. Emerson to an Army post at Rock Island, Illinois. A year or so later, Emerson was sent to Fort Snelling, in that portion of Wisconsin Territory which later became a part of the state of Minnesota. Scott went along as Dr. Emerson's house servant. In 1836, the surgeon bought a slave woman named Harriet from a Major Taliaferro. That same year, Scott obtained the permission of Dr. Emerson to marry Harriet, and the couple had a child whom they named Eliza. In 1838, Dr. Emerson returned to St. Louis and brought Dred Scott and his family with him. Six years later, the surgeon died, leaving Scott to his widow, Mrs. Irene Sanford Emerson. When she moved to New York in the mid-1840's, Mrs. Emerson left Scott with Henry and Taylor Blow, sons of Scott's original owner.

Henry Blow, a lawyer and well-to-do businessman, was active in the antislavery movement. In 1846, he helped finance a case in the Missouri courts to win Scott's freedom. Why was it necessary to go to court? Mrs. Emerson did not believe in slavery and could have signed papers manumitting (freeing) Scott. But she decided to go along with Henry Blow and other antislavery men who wanted a court decision on the rights of a slave who had lived in free territory. (Slavery had been prohibited in Wisconsin Territory since 1820.) Scott's case was listed in court as *Scott, a Man of Color, v. Emerson.*

Dred Scott's lawyers argued that the years he had spent in free territory made him a free man. The lower court ruled in Scott's favor. However, the lawyers on both sides wanted a ruling from a higher court, which would subsequently win the case national attention. So the Dred Scott case was appealed, and the Missouri Supreme Court reversed the ruling of the lower court. It held that Scott had voluntarily returned from free territory to Missouri and, as a resident of Missouri, he was therefore still a slave.

The Scott case dragged through the state courts for six years,

[4]

Henry T. Blow, the son of Peter Blow, Scott's first owner, was a well-to-do St. Louis lawyer and businessman. He helped finance a suit in the Missouri courts to free Scott. (Culver Pictures)

and the Missouri Supreme Court did not hand down its decision until 1852. During those six years, Texas had become a state in the Union, and the United States had won a huge tract of territory from Mexico. These events made even more critical and prickly the questions raised by *Scott, a Man of Color, v. Emerson:* Did a slave owner have the right to take his slaves into the territories of the United States? Could Congress prohibit slavery in the territories? A great many people thought, or at least hoped, that these questions had been settled in 1820.

The Background of a "Peculiar Institution" —Slavery

During the early 1800's, the slave-owning cotton planters of the South looked eagerly to the new territory in the Mississippi and Missouri valleys. Cotton growing wore out the soil, and newer, fresher land was needed every few years. But the Southern planters' push westward was bound to bring them in conflict with the free-soil men who opposed the spread of slavery and the plantation system. The latter wanted the western territories to become the home of small farmers and workers from the North.

The first clash came in 1819, when Missouri sought admission to the Union as a slave state. Free-soil men objected, and tension between the North and South built up dangerously. With Congress hopelessly deadlocked, Representative Henry Clay of Kentucky offered his Missouri Compromise of 1820. It provided for the admission of Missouri as a slave state, and Maine as a free state. There were now twelve slave and twelve free states in the Union, and the balance of power between the North and South was maintained. The compromise also banned slavery north of the parallel 36° 30′, the southern boundary of Missouri. (The ban did not apply to that state, however.) By this action, Congress appeared to have settled the question of its right to prohibit slavery in the territories. But, later, southerners would heatedly deny that Congress had such a right.

Clay's compromise cooled tempers — but not for long. The next clash in Congress did not directly involve slavery, but that institution had much to do with it. The slave-owning agricultural South had few factories. So it wanted to buy factory-made goods from England, which in turn bought much of the South's cotton and other products. But the North, which was becoming an industrial region, wanted to protect its factories from the competition of English goods. The Tariff

This cartoon pictured President Andrew Jackson in 1832 as "King Andrew the First," a tyrant who trampled on the Constitution and the Supreme Court. The next year, when the South Carolina legislature declared tariff acts null and void and asserted a state's right to secede from the Union, the tough-minded Jackson threatened to send troops to South Carolina. His vigorous action quieted secession talk for almost fifteen years. (New York Historical Society)

Act of 1828 put a high duty (tax) on foreign-made goods and sharply raised the prices that southerners had to pay for imported articles. They denounced the measure as a "Tariff of Abominations," and a new tariff was passed by Congress in 1832. While the bill lowered the duties on many products, the South Carolina leader, Vice-President John C. Calhoun, was not satisfied. He fought the new tariff with his doctrine of nullification. This doctrine declared, first, that any state had the right to rule null and void any act of Congress which injured the state and thereby violated the federal Constitution, and, second, that the Constitution itself was merely an agreement under which a state could leave the Union any time it felt like doing so.

Accordingly, the South Carolina legislature passed an ordinance declaring the Tariffs of 1828 and 1832 null and void. Then Calhoun resigned the Vice-Presidency and entered the Senate to lead the fight for nullification and states' rights. President Andrew Jackson bluntly declared that the Constitution had been ratified by all the states to form a more perfect Union. No state, he insisted, had the right to break away from that Union. No state, he added, could decide for itself which laws it would obey. Jackson backed up his stern words by threatening to send troops to South Carolina and to hang Calhoun. The President was, however, ready to accept a compromise, and Henry Clay was ready to help work one out. The tariff rates were lowered, and South Carolina abolished its ordinance of nullification. This served to quiet down southern talk of states' rights and secession for about fifteen years. But the disturbed Jackson told a friend that the tariff clash was only a pretext, an excuse, for nullification. He said the real object of Calhoun and his followers was disunion. He gloomily predicted that agitation for secession would continue, and that the "next pretext will be the Negro, or slavery, question."

In the mid-1830's, attacks on slavery as a crime began to increase, and the South rallied to defend its "peculiar institution." Earlier, there had been scores of southern antislavery societies that favored the grad-

The South's champion, gaunt, hoarse-voiced Senator John C. Calhoun, answered abolitionist attacks on slavery by declaring that it "is, instead of an evil, a good — a positive good." Later, he would insist that "slavery follows the flag" and could not be kept out of any territory of the United States. (National Archives)

ual emancipation of slaves. Now they disappeared, and the South listened to Calhoun. The gaunt senator, his eyes blazing, his voice harsh, told the Senate that slavery "is, instead of an evil, a good — a positive good." But, as he studied census reports, Calhoun could see a deadly threat to the South and to slavery from the new, free states in the Northwest. In Illinois, for example, the population jumped from 53,000 in 1820 to 472,000 in 1840. The population of Indiana increased from 157,000 in 1820 to 476,000 in 1840. But the population of the wealthiest southern state, Virginia, remained practically stationary from 1820 to 1840. In the House of Representatives, where each state's number of representatives is based on its population, the South was heavily outnumbered. Only in the Senate, where each state has two senators, could the South hold its own — and only then if the

Ralph Waldo Emerson, famous poet, essayist and foe of slavery, opposed the conquest of Mexican territory. "Mexico will poison us," he warned, and his warning soon proved frighteningly accurate. (Culver Pictures)

number of slave and free states remained fairly evenly balanced. Then, in 1845, Texas was admitted to the Union, and the Mexican War soon followed. Nothing was the same after that.

Senator Calhoun had favored the admission of Texas to the Union. But he feared that the conquest of Mexican territory would bring a dangerous quarrel between slavery and free-soil forces in Congress. "Mexico is forbidden fruit," he wrote. "The penalty of eating it would be to subject our institutions to political death." The famous essayist and foe of slavery Ralph Waldo Emerson agreed with Calhoun — at least on this one point. Said Emerson: "Mexico will poison us."

The peace treaty with Mexico gave New Mexico, including Arizona and Upper California, to the United States. Soon after this, the question of slavery in the new territories arose. A northern Democrat, Representative David Wilmot of Pennsylvania, introduced a proviso in the House. It declared that no territory obtained from Mexico should ever be open to slavery. The Wilmot Proviso was passed by the House, but southern Democrats defeated it in the Senate. They angrily denied that the Missouri Compromise of 1820 had settled the question of Congress's right to ban slavery in the territories. "Slav-

[10]

While Lincoln was a member of Congress in 1847-49, he saw Negroes sold at slave markets like this one in the District of Columbia. Near the end of his term in the House, Lincoln introduced a resolution, which was defeated, to provide for the gradual emancipation of slaves in the district. (National Park Service)

ery follows the flag," growled Calhoun, and contended that the institution could not be kept out of a territory. The Virginia legislature passed a resolution declaring that Congress had no authority over slavery.

As bitterness swept through Congress and the country, President James K. Polk watched and worried. The tough-minded Polk had led the fight to win Mexican territory. Now he seemed rather appalled by his handiwork. He wrote in his diary: "The slavery question is assuming a fearful and most important aspect." He added that if the Wilmot Proviso was pushed in Congress, "it cannot fail to destroy the Democratic party, if it does not ultimately threaten the Union itself."

"Free Soil" and Clay's Compromise of 1850

The fight over the Wilmot Proviso led to the formation of a strong third party in the 1848 Presidential campaign. New York Democrats, known as "Barnburners," joined the "conscience" (antislavery) Whigs and members of the Liberty party to form the Free-Soil party. It nominated former President Martin Van Buren and proclaimed: "We inscribe on our banner Free Soil, Free Speech, Free Labor and Free Men."

The Whigs tried to avoid the slavery question by nominating the Mexican War hero General Zachary Taylor for President. He had always kept his opinions on slavery and other political questions to himself. The Democrats nominated Lewis Cass of Michigan. He opposed the Wilmot Proviso and favored the doctrine of squatter sovereignty to solve the problem of slavery in the territories. This meant that the voters in each territory should decide whether or not they wanted slavery. The Democrats hoped that this proposal would cool the slavery quarrel and keep it from splitting the party.

[12]

In the election, the Free-Soilers took enough votes away from Cass to swing the Presidency to Taylor. They had shown both the Whigs and Democrats that a growing number of people were becoming active opponents of slavery. Unfortunately, Whig and Democratic leaders paid little attention.

With Taylor in the White House, the southern Democrats, led by Calhoun, made a last great effort to control Congress. The battle lines were drawn when California sought to enter the Union as a free state in 1849. Also involved was the future of the New Mexico and Utah territories. Supporters of the Wilmot Proviso clashed head on with Calhoun who grimly kept insisting that "slavery follows the flag." Again, the Union seemed about to split into warring sections. Calhoun's followers issued a bitter Southern Address, which charged that the North was out to ruin the South. Senator Sam Houston of Texas stood alone in refusing to sign the address. He said "it would excite the Southern people and drive them further on the road to separation from their Northern friends." Houston fought for the Union, as his good friend Andrew Jackson had done in 1833. Southern secessionists called Houston a traitor to the South. To this charge, he eloquently replied that he knew "neither North nor South," but "only the

When the quarrel over slavery threatened to split the Union, Senator Henry Clay offered his Compromise of 1850. A leading supporter of the compromise was Senator Sam Houston, right, the hero of Texas' war for independence from Mexico. Accused of being a traitor to the South, Houston said he knew "neither North nor South," but "only the Union." This courageous stand finally cost him his seat in the U.S. Senate. (Texas State Capitol, Austin)

Advertisements illustrated with the figure of a running Negro appeared frequently in newspapers. The owner of this slave warns anyone who might help the runaway that "the law will be enforced." This law, the Fugitive Slave Act, aroused bitter opposition and caused many people to help the "underground railroad" smuggle slaves to safety in Canada. (Washington Evening Star)

Union." He further said that in the Senate he was a "representative of the whole American people," and he believed the people of Texas would support him "for they are true to the Union." Texans honored Houston as the leader in their war for independence in 1836, and as first President of the Republic of Texas. But now his stand for the Union cost him many supporters. While southerners ranted against him in the Senate, Houston would calmly take out his knife and whittle on a pine stick.

In 1850, as in 1820 and 1833, the smiling, persuasive Henry Clay came up with another compromise. Houston was among the first senators to back the compromise, and was again berated by Texans. Pleading for Clay's proposals, Houston did not dodge the threat of disunion. "I wish," he said, "if this Union *must* be dissolved, that its ruins may be the monument of my grave." Under Clay's Compromise of 1850, California would be admitted as a free state, while settlers in New

[14]

Mexico and Utah would be allowed to decide whether to be slave or free (a first trial for squatter sovereignty). The slave trade in the District of Columbia would be abolished, but to soothe the South, a stronger Fugitive Slave Act would speed the return of runaway slaves to their masters.

Senator Daniel Webster of Massachusetts joined Clay in getting Congress to pass the compromise. In doing so, they had to beat down the resistance of antislavery Senators Salmon P. Chase of Ohio and William H. Seward of New York, as well as the defiant Calhoun. The dying Calhoun had to have a colleague read his speech on the floor. He warned the South that it no longer had "any adequate means of protecting itself against . . . encroachment and oppression." He said the North must cease its propaganda against slavery. Otherwise, "let the states . . . part in peace."

Senator Webster's famous and powerful speech of March 7 saved the compromise. Echoing the words of Houston, Webster said he spoke for the Union, "not as a Massachusetts man, nor a Northern man, but as an American." In backing the compromise, particularly the Fugitive Slave Act, Webster sacrificed his popularity and killed his chances for the Presidency. His was one of the greatest speeches ever made in the Senate. For a moment, the "poison" of the Mexican War seemed to have been purged from Congress.

When Clay died in 1852, the Compromise of 1850 appeared still to be keeping the country calm. But many northerners refused to obey the Fugitive Slave Act. They helped the "underground railroad" smuggle runaway slaves across free states and into Canada. The Fugitive Slave Act also inspired Harriet Beecher Stowe to write *Uncle Tom's Cabin*. Published in 1852, it was the most influential piece of writing that ever appeared against slavery. The book was no one-sided attack on slavery. But foes of the "peculiar institution" remembered those parts that supported their arguments.

In 1852, both the Democratic and Whig parties failed to nominate

This daguerreotype, made in 1846, the year he was elected to Congress, is the earliest photograph of Lincoln. After serving one unsuccessful term in Congress, Lincoln returned to his law practice, feeling that his political career was ended. He was jolted back into politics when his long-time political foe, Senator Stephen A. Douglas, rammed the Kansas-Nebraska Act through Congress in 1854. (Library of Congress)

Aroused by the Fugitive Slave Act, Harriet Beecher Stowe wrote Uncle Tom's Cabin, the most effective attack ever made on slavery. (Culver Pictures)

a Presidential candidate who would give the nation the leadership it sorely needed. Sam Houston's stand for the Compromise of 1850 had won him support among Whigs and Democrats. Charles Sumner, the fiery, antislavery senator from Massachusetts, talked with Houston and was pleasantly surprised. "With him," said Sumner, "the anti-slavery interests would stand better than with any other man." But stubborn southern Democrats and frightened Whigs were in no mood to consider the independent, plain-speaking Houston. Instead, the Democrats nominated Franklin Pierce of New Hampshire, a northerner with southern sympathies. He was a follower, not a leader. The Whigs nominated another Mexican War hero, General Winfield Scott, a good Army officer but nothing more than that. Pierce had little trouble winning the election. His victory was hailed as a victory for the Compromise of 1850, but the era of good feeling was not to last long.

The Kansas-Nebraska Act of 1854

In 1854, the nation was jolted out of its Compromise of 1850 mood by the passage of the Kansas-Nebraska Act. It was the work of Senator Stephen A. Douglas of Illinois, who was called the Little Giant by his friends and "a steam engine in britches" by his foes. For months, southerners in Congress had blocked every effort to organize the Nebraska Territory, which was north of the line drawn by the Missouri Compromise of 1820 and thus barred to slavery. Declaring war on the Compromise of 1820, the South insisted that Congress had no power to ban slavery in this territory.

Douglas sought to break the deadlock by proposing that the doctrine of squatter sovereignty be applied to Nebraska. He also agreed to divide the territory into Kansas and Nebraska, with Kansas expected to become a slave state and Nebraska a free one. This proposal, by implication, repealed the Missouri Compromise. But southern fire-eaters demanded that Douglas spell it out for all to see. So Douglas amended his bill to repeal the Missouri Compromise of 1820.

Senator Sam Houston was the lone southerner to oppose the bill. Denouncing him, the Richmond *Enquirer* sputtered, "Nothing can justify such treachery." Houston in the Senate stood his ground. "I ask again," he said, "what benefit is to result to the South from this measure? . . . Will it secure these territories to the South? No, sir, not at all. Instead, it furnishes those in the North who are enemies of the South, with efficient weapons." Houston raised his hand and pointed to the symbolic eagle above the chair of the presiding officer. It was draped in black to mourn the deaths of Clay and Webster. He asked "if this badge of mourning also represents a fearful omen of future calamities which await our nation in event this bill should become law. . . . I adjure you, harmonize and preserve this nation. . . . Give us peace!"

There was to be no peace for the nation or for Houston. The bill passed, and Texas declared Houston's career as a United States senator at an end. In Washington, Democratic cannon boomed the news of the Kansas-Nebraska victory. Senator Chase said to Senator Sumner: "They celebrate a present victory, but the echoes they awake shall never rest until slavery itself shall die." The Kansas-Nebraska Act was to bring death to the Whig party and cause a new party, the Republican, to come on the political scene.

Foes accused Douglas of favoring the South in order to win the Presidential nomination in 1856. Actually, he was anxious to organize the Nebraska Territory so that a railroad could be built through it from Chicago to the Pacific Coast. Douglas also felt that slavery would never really take hold in either Kansas or Nebraska because the climate there was not suited to slave-cultivated crops. The Little Giant had a relaxed attitude toward slavery, saying he did not care whether "it was voted up or down."

[18]

The Kansas-Nebraska Act infuriated the North and Northwest. It aroused all the hates and fears that the Compromise of 1850 had quieted for a few years. For the first time, a territory that had been closed to slavery was opened to it. Hundreds of mass meetings were called to denounce Douglas. Among the men who took to the speaker's platform in these meetings was an Illinois lawyer, Abraham Lincoln. He had served one term as a Whig congressman, but his opposition to the Mexican War had ended his chances for reelection. Lincoln had gone back to his Springfield law practice and paid little attention to politics. But now he forgot his law books and immediately plunged into the fight against the Kansas-Nebraska Act.

Slavery *v.* Free Soil in "Bleeding Kansas"

At Peoria, Illinois, on October 16, 1854, Abraham Lincoln, for the first time, denounced slavery in a public speech. His was the clearest statement of the free-soil attitude toward slavery that anyone had yet made. Lincoln insisted that he had no desire to interfere with slavery in the South. "If all earthly power were given me, I should not know what to do as to the existing institution. . . ." But because slavery was wrong, he added, it must not be allowed to spread into the territories. Then, he proceeded to attack Douglas' popular-sovereignty doctrine. It was false, he said, because the question of slavery in the territories was the business of all the people, not just the people in Kansas and Nebraska.

While Lincoln was busy dealing with the big issue of the day, the Whig party, which tried to avoid it, was tottering toward its grave. The new Republican party was seeking to win a nationwide following. It was composed of a strange assortment of often-quarreling Free-Soilers, antislavery Whigs, anti-Nebraska Democrats, abolitionists, and so-called "Know-Nothings." The Know-Nothings were a secret, anti-foreign, anti-Catholic organization that feared the thousands of immigrants from Europe would take the jobs of American workers. Members were initiated with great secrecy and swore never to reveal the "mysteries" of the organization. Outsiders attempting to obtain information were told "I know nothing about it." As a result, the organization was dubbed the Know-Nothing movement.

While proslavery and antislavery men clashed in "bleeding Kansas," sharp-tongued Senator Charles Sumner made a speech bitterly attacking Senator Andrew Butler of South Carolina. Three days later, Representative Preston Brooks, a kinsman of Butler's, entered the Senate and beat Sumner insensible with a cane. Called a bully in the North and a hero in the South, Brooks resigned from the House, but was reelected by defiant South Carolinians. (New York Public Library, Prints Division)

In 1855 and 1856, Kansas became a battleground as both slavery and free-soil men rushed to the territory. "Border ruffians" from Missouri swarmed into Kansas and set up a proslavery government at Lecompton. Free-soil men organized a rival government at Topeka. President Pierce followed the lead of his southern advisers and recognized the Lecompton government. The House backed the government in Topeka, but the Senate opposed it. The deadlock continued in Congress while civil war raged in Kansas. In thirteen months, more than two hundred men were killed in "bleeding Kansas."

The Ostend Manifesto and the Election of 1856

While the excitement over Kansas was at a boil, the acid-tongued Senator Charles Sumner spoke in the Senate. During his speech, he attacked Senator Andrew Butler of South Carolina, who was not in the Senate chamber. Three days later, Representative Preston Brooks, a kinsman of Butler's, entered the Senate and beat Senator Sumner into insensibility with a cane. The North was enraged by the attack, while the South hailed Brooks as a hero. Brooks sent an apology to the Senate and resigned his seat in the House, but was reelected by defiant South Carolinians.

Congress now became a battleground as threats and insults volleyed back and forth. Representative Keitt of South Carolina called Representative Crow of Pennsylvania a "black Republican puppy," touching off a fistfight involving a dozen members of the House. In Congress and out, northerners and southerners seemed not to speak the same language. The art of compromise, of friendly persuasion, was fast disappearing. Southern hotheads were ready to take the South out of the Union if they could not have their way. In addition, fire-eating abolitionists were out to smash slavery no matter what happened to the Union. Time was running out for the moderate, middle-of-the-road men who hoped to hold the Union together. It was later than anyone thought.

The anger and suspicion of abolitionists and Free-Soilers were heightened by the Ostend Manifesto, a rash statement issued by the United States ministers to Britain, Spain, and France, who met at Ostend, Belgium. They advised President Pierce that the United States should buy Cuba from Spain, because it was thought that Cuba was indispensable for the security of slavery. If Spain did not sell, the ministers declared, the United States should take the island by force.

The Republican party, which held its first national convention in Philadelphia in 1856, was quick to pounce on the Ostend Manifesto. It was called "the highwayman's plea that might makes right." The Republican platform of promises to the voters upheld the Missouri Compromise, opposed the spread of slavery to the territories, and demanded the admission of Kansas as a free state. For President, the Republicans nominated John C. Frémont, "the Pathfinder" of the Far West and son-in-law of ex-Senator Thomas Hart Benton of Missouri. Their slogan was "Free soil, free speech, free men and Frémont."

The Democratic party, firmly controlled by southerners, nominated another northern man with southern sympathies — James Buchanan of Pennsylvania. He said he personally disliked slavery, but felt that abolitionists were a threat to the Union. He seemed not to be aware that thousands of other people were becoming increasingly angered by attempts to push slavery into the western territories.

The contest between Buchanan and Frémont was complicated by a third-party candidate. Former President Millard Fillmore was backed by the American party, a mixture of ex-Whigs and immigrant-hating Know-Nothings. At Galena, Illinois, on July 23, Lincoln boldly faced the charge by Fillmore that the election of Frémont would cause the

The American party Presidential candidate, Millard Fillmore, is called the "right man in the right place," as he stands between John C. Frémont, candidate of the new Republican party, and James Buchanan, the Democratic candidate. Both Fillmore and Buchanan warned that Frémont's election would cause the South to secede. Lincoln's answer was: "We won't dissolve the Union, and you shan't." (New York Historical Society)

South to secede from the Union. "All this talk about dissolution of the Union is humbug — nothing but folly," said Lincoln. "We won't dissolve the Union, and you shan't."

Yet many prominent men who opposed slavery still feared that Frémont's election would bring disunion. Frémont's father-in-law, combative Tom Benton, had lost his seat in the Senate because of his free-soil views. Still full of fight, Benton in 1852 won a seat in the House, where he charged that the Kansas-Nebraska Act was a clumsy attempt to sneak slavery into the territories. This stand cost him his seat in the House, but it did not silence him. Despite his strong free-soil views, Benton opposed his son-in-law. He said the Republican movement was accentuating the hostility between the two sections. "We are treading," he warned, "upon a volcano that is liable at any moment to burst forth and overwhelm the nation."

Millard Fillmore got the support of many middle-of-the-road men who were worried by the growing power of the Republican party. The Democratic party did all it could to feed their fears. They warned voters that the Republican party was sectional and had strength only in the North. If it won, the nation would be plunged into disunion and war. Many southern newspapers flatly warned that Frémont's election would bring disunion. The Charleston *Mercury* commented that his election "will be and ought to be the knell of the Union."

Lincoln tried hard to keep voters in Illinois from "throwing away" their votes on Fillmore. His efforts were in vain. Buchanan won Illinois because of the three-way split in the vote. In the nation, Buchanan polled fewer popular votes than Frémont and Fillmore combined. But Buchanan got a majority of the electoral votes and won the Presidency.

In its first Presidential election, the Republican party had done surprisingly well, winning all the states of the Northeast. Although Buchanan won his home state, Pennsylvania, as well as New Jersey, Indiana, Illinois, and California, his main strength was in the South. Buchanan had emphasized that the Democratic party, unlike the Republican, spoke for the Union, the whole nation. But he was elected without the support of one powerful section of the country. This result worried many middle-of-the-roaders. Both parties were becoming sectional. Would this rise of sectionalism be the forerunner of disunion and war?

Dred Scott v. Sandford

While the slavery controversy was sharpening tempers to a fine edge, Dred Scott puttered around on one odd job and another. Most of the time, he had been held by the sheriff of the county, who hired him out for jobs in the neighborhood. His owner, Mrs. Emerson, paid little attention to him. Scott was a forgotten man. Then, in 1850, Mrs. Emerson married Dr. Calvin C. Chaffee, an abolitionist congressman from Massachusetts, and Scott suddenly became important again. Chaffee obviously did not want to own a slave. But, instead of freeing him, Chaffee decided to use Scott to get a ruling from the Supreme Court of the United States on the rights of a slave who had lived in free territory. Since Chaffee did not want to be sued by Scott's lawyers, he "sold" the slave to Mrs. Emerson's brother, John F. A. Sanford of New York.

Under the Constitution, suits between "citizens of different states" are tried in federal court. So in order to get their case into federal court, Scott's lawyers brought suit in Missouri, alleging that Scott was a citizen of Missouri, and Sanford a citizen of New York. Sanford's lawyers defended the suit in federal circuit court in Missouri, and Scott's lawyers won the first point. The court held that Scott was a citizen of Missouri and had the right to sue in federal court. But the court went on to decide that, under Missouri law, Scott was still a slave. Scott's lawyers appealed the case to the Supreme Court of the United States. Both sides wanted a ruling from the Court on Congress's power to ban slavery in the territories, as was done in the Missouri Compromise in 1820.

Chief Justice Roger Brooke Taney believed that the Supreme Court could settle the slavery question once and for all. Seldom in history has a man made a more tragic miscalculation. Taney's opinion so enraged people that his long years of brilliant service as Chief Justice were largely forgotten. (Culver Pictures)

The case of *Dred Scott v. Sandford* reached the Supreme Court early in 1856. (The name of the defendant, John F. A. Sanford, was misspelled by the clerk — the first of several mistakes made by persons involved in this case. In fact, everybody in the case seemed to have a childlike faith that a Court decision would settle the bothersome slavery problem.)

After hearing the arguments of opposing lawyers, the justices held a conference to discuss the case in May of 1856. The majority decided that the decision of the circuit court in Missouri should be upheld on the basis of an 1851 case, *Strader v. Graham.* This case involved the same issue as that in *Dred Scott v. Sandford:* Do slaves whose Kentucky owner allowed them to work in Ohio, a free state, thereby win their freedom? The Supreme Court had held that their rights were dependent on the laws of the state they came from (Kentucky), not on the laws of Ohio. Thus, when the slaves had returned to Kentucky, they again became the property of their owner. By following the decision in *Strader v. Graham,* the Court would avoid the question of Congress's power over slavery in the territories. The Dred Scott case already had aroused a lot of interest. Indeed, it was becoming a hot potato, and the majority of the justices were planning to handle it with thick mittens.

At this point, however, Justice John McLean of Ohio announced that he was going to write a dissenting opinion. In it, he would declare Scott a free man and uphold Congress's power over slavery. McLean's stand obviously was caused by an attack of Presidential fever. He had been a contender for the Whig Presidential nomination in 1852. Later, he became a Republican and lost that party's Presidential nomination to Frémont in 1856. Although he was seventy-two, McLean still hoped to win the Republican nomination in 1860, and a strong dissent in the Dred Scott case would win him a lot of support. Justice Benjamin R. Curtis, a Whig from Massachusetts, also jolted the other justices by announcing that he, too, would dissent. The McLean-Curtis announcements caused the Court majority to delay action on the case until after the 1856 Presidential election. The other seven members of the Court were all Democrats, and five were from slave states: Chief Justice Taney, from Maryland; Justices James M. Wayne, Georgia; John Catron, Tennessee; Peter V. Daniel, Virginia; and John A. Campbell, Alabama. The two northern Democrats were Justices Samuel Nelson of New York and Robert C. Grier of Pennsylvania.

[27]

President James Buchanan, a northerner with southern sympathies, also felt that a Supreme Court decision denying Congress's power over slavery in the territories would settle the question. He, too, sadly underestimated the strength and bitterness of the antislavery feeling in the nation. (National Archives)

President Buchanan Takes a Hand

After the election, the case was again taken up by the Court. At this time, however, there was a delay because of the sickness of one justice. Day by day, interest in the case built up until *Dred Scott v. Sandford* was about the only thing people discussed. Proslavery congressmen kept busy trying to influence southern members of the Court to hand down a decision protecting slavery. Antislavery newspapers grumbled that no good could come from a Court that was controlled by southern Democrats and slave owners. The hot potato was getting hotter. At length President-elect James Buchanan decided to take a hand in the case. Congress still was deadlocked over Kansas, and Buchanan knew that he soon would have to do something about it. A decision by the Court limiting Congress's power over slavery might help him out. So the President-elect took the unusual and not exactly proper step of writing to his good friend on the Court, Justice Catron. He asked Catron whether the Court would hand down a decision before the Presidential inaugural on March 4. Catron replied that the case would be decided in February, but the decision "would not help" because the question of Congress's power over slavery would not be determined.

Meanwhile, Justice Wayne decided that, since McLean and Curtis still planned to dissent, the Court majority should declare that Congress had no power over slavery anywhere. Taney and the other southern justices came around to Wayne's view. But Grier wanted more time to think it over. So Catron decided to write his friend James Buchanan and ask him to use some influence on Grier. Buchanan did write to Grier, and the justice replied, in an unusual and not exactly proper letter. He told the President-elect: "We fully appreciate and concur in your views as to the desirableness at this time of having an expression from the Court on this troublesome question." Grier went on to explain that the Court majority at first had merely intended to uphold the decision of the circuit court. "But it appeared," he added, "that our brothers who dissented from the majority, especially Justice McLean, were determined to come out with a long and labored dissent. . . ." Thus, wrote Grier, the majority decided to rule on the Missouri Compromise and Congress's power over slavery: "There will therefore be six, if not seven (perhaps Nelson will remain neutral)

[29]

who will decide the Compromise law of 1820 to be of non-effect. But the opinions will not be delivered before Friday the 6th of March. We will not let any others of our brethren know anything about the cause of our anxiety to produce this result, and though contrary to our usual practice, we have thought it due to you to state to you in candor and confidence the real state of the matter."

With Grier's letter in his pocket, Buchanan then made a great show of being a good sport about the Dred Scott case. In his inaugural address on March 4, he said that the question of slavery in the territories "is a judicial question which legitimately belongs to the Supreme Court of the United States before whom it is now pending. . . . To their decision, in common with all good citizens, I shall cheerfully submit, whatever that may be."

As predicted by Justice Grier, Nelson remained neutral. He read an opinion upholding the circuit court decision and dodged the question of whether Scott was a citizen or whether the Missouri Compromise was constitutional. The majority opinion of the Court was delivered by Chief Justice Taney. The other four southern justices and Grier supported it. McLean and Curtis dissented.

Taney's opinion slammed the door on Scott in no uncertain language. He held that since Negroes were not citizens at the time of the writing of the Declaration of Independence and the Constitution, Dred Scott was not a citizen of Missouri or any state. Thus, Scott was not entitled to sue Sanford in federal court, and his case must, therefore, be dismissed. "It is difficult," Taney declared, "at this day to realize the state of public opinion in relation to that unfortunate race, which prevailed . . . at the time of the Declaration of Independence, and when the Constitution of the United States was framed and adopted. . . . They had for more than a century been regarded as beings of an inferior order, and altogether unfit to associate with the white race, either in social or political relations; and so far inferior, that they had no rights which the white man was bound to respect. . . ."

[30]

If Taney had ended his opinion here, the outcry against the Court would not have been so loud. But Taney did not stop. He went on to say that even if Scott had the right to sue, he would lose his case. He would lose because, even though he had lived in free territory, this did not make him a free man. Taney then explained that the Fifth Amendment provides that no person may be deprived of his property without due process of law. Thus, argued Taney, the Missouri Compromise, which prohibited slavery in Wisconsin Territory, was unconstitutional because it denied a slave owner the right to take his property there without running the risk of losing it. ". . . Neither Dred Scott himself, nor any of his family, were made free by being carried into this territory; even if they had been carried there by the owner with the intention of becoming a permanent resident." Congress, Taney concluded, could not keep slavery out of any territory of the United States. It would also follow that a territorial legislature could not keep slavery out either.

Since Taney had started out by saying that Scott had no right to sue in federal court, it was not necessary for him to rule on the constitutionality of the Missouri Compromise. Furthermore, Congress had repealed the compromise three years earlier when it passed the Kansas-Nebraska Act. In attempting to settle the slavery question once and for all, Taney covered too much ground. He was really asking for trouble.

Justice Wayne read a short opinion in which he agreed with Taney on all points. Then he went on rather plaintively to argue: "The case involves private rights of value, and constitutional principles of the highest importance, about which there has been such a difference of opinion that the peace and harmony of the country required the settlement of them by judicial decision." In arguing that the Court had to act for "the peace and harmony of the country," Wayne, as well as Taney and Buchanan, sadly misjudged the temper of the free-soil and antislavery forces in the nation.

[31]

In their dissenting opinions, both McLean and Curtis declared that Scott was a citizen and a free man, and the Missouri Compromise was constitutional. In his opinion, Curtis took dead aim at Taney. He said the Court majority had no right to rule on the constitutionality of the Missouri Compromise after it had declared Scott had no right to sue in federal court. He added that Taney's opinion was not binding upon him or anyone else.

The opinions of McLean and Curtis were published by the newspapers long before Taney's majority decision was made public. Curtis, who had left Washington and gone home, now heard that Taney was rewriting his opinion to reply to Curtis' dissent. There followed an ill-tempered exchange of letters between Curtis and Taney. The Chief Justice refused to send Curtis a copy of his opinion, and Curtis charged that he was busy rewriting it. A month later, Taney replied and angrily denied that he had changed any fact in his opinion. When Curtis got a copy, he marked dozens of changes that he said Taney had made after he had read the opinion in Court.

Not long after his quarrel with Taney, Curtis resigned from the Court, giving as his reason the low salary of an associate justice. Privately, Curtis told friends that he could not "again feel confidence in the Court and that willingness to cooperate with them which is essential to the satisfactory discharge of my duties." This, tragically, was the attitude of many people in the North and South. They were forgetting the meaning of words like "cooperate" and "compromise." The poison of the Mexican War was at work in the nation. It might be said that the Supreme Court hoped to purge the nation. But its cure, the Dred Scott decision, proved worse than the disease.

The Reaction—"This Wicked and False Judgment"

Taney's opinion sent explosions of anger ricocheting through the North and Northwest (or Midwest, as it is known today). Democrats deserted their party and joined the Republicans. Antislavery newspapers charged that the Supreme Court decision was the final act in a plot to spread slavery throughout the Union. Abraham Lincoln later was to make shrewd use of this fear that slavery might spread into every part of the nation. At the same time, fire-eating southerners demanded that the Dred Scott decision be followed to the letter and that all territories be opened to slavery.

Chief Justice Taney, now the target of much abuse, was himself a slave owner who had freed all of his slaves except two, whom he cared for because they were too old to work. At this time, Taney was still suffering from the shock of the deaths of his wife and their last child, a beautiful daughter. Taney had been a highly respected Chief Justice since 1836, but now all of his past service was forgotten by his critics. The New York *Tribune* snapped: "The Court has rushed into politics, voluntarily and without other purpose than to preserve the cause of slavery.... Their cunning chief led the van...." The newspaper went on to call the decision "this wicked and false judgment," and said that it was "entitled to just as much moral weight as would be the judgment of a majority of those congregated in a Washington barroom." William Cullen Bryant's New York *Evening Post* said that "if this decision shall stand for law" the nation's flag "should be dyed black, and its device should be the whip and the fetter...." Even the conservative *New York Times* warned that "the circumstances attending the present decision have done much to divest it of moral authority and to impair the confidence of the country."

Senator Seward could not have known it at the time, but he made

Senator William H. Seward of New York ridiculed President Buchanan's promise to "cheerfully submit" to the Supreme Court's Dred Scott decision, "whatever it may be." He charged that Buchanan knew in advance that the Court would rule against Scott, and that the President had schemed with the Court "to hang the millstone of slavery on the neck of the people of Kansas. . . ." (National Park Service)

a shrewd guess that Buchanan knew in advance of the Court's decision. He ridiculed the President's promise to "cheerfully submit" to the decision "whatever that may be." He charged that Buchanan had plotted with the Court "to hang the millstone of slavery on the neck of the people of Kansas. . . ." President Buchanan, a charming but bumbling man, thought that a Court decision could settle the slavery problem. But slavery was like a loaded gun, and Buchanan was the man who "didn't know it was loaded."

For the second time in the nation's history, the Supreme Court had ruled an act of Congress unconstitutional. Chief Justice John Marshall handed down the first such decision in the famous case of *Marbury v. Madison.* This had caused a row, but it in no way compared with the uproar touched off by *Dred Scott v. Sandford.* The

Court was not destroyed by the Dred Scott decision, but for a good many years after that March day in 1857, the Court had little to say about the affairs of the nation. The Court lived, but the evil it had done lived on and on. Decades later, Chief Justice Charles Evans Hughes would declare that the Court suffered from a "self-inflicted wound" and that the decision was a "public calamity."

A few days after the Court's decision, Scott's owner manumitted him, and he continued, as before, to work on odd jobs. Scott's days were calm, but the same could not be said for many other people who had become involved in the Dred Scott decision. Scott still could not understand what all "the fuss" was about. But the "fuss" over him changed the lives of many important men: President Buchanan, Chief Justice Taney, Stephen Douglas, and Abraham Lincoln. The man that Scott's case helped the most was Lincoln.

The Dred Scott decision appeared to make a shambles of Senator Douglas' popular-sovereignty principle. It also apparently blocked the Republican drive to keep slavery from spreading to new territories. Douglas coolly said that popular sovereignty was still alive. It was true, he admitted, that a person could take slaves into a territory. But that was a "barren and worthless right" unless the voters of a territory passed local laws to protect slavery. Lincoln just as coolly declared that "the Court that made it [the decision] has often overruled its own decisions, and we shall do what we can to have it overrule this. We offer no *resistance* to it."

Encouraged by the Dred Scott decision, President Buchanan urged Congress to approve the proslavery constitution for Kansas, which had been written at Lecompton. Douglas angrily charged that the Lecompton "fraud" was opposed by a majority of the voters of Kansas and made a mockery of popular sovereignty. He rallied enough support from northern Democrats and Republicans to defeat the constitution in the House of Representatives.

Now Douglas was under attack from Buchanan and his southern

friends. He also had to run against Lincoln in the 1858 senatorial campaign in Illinois. Accepting the nomination for the Senate, Lincoln declared: " 'A house divided against itself cannot stand.' I believe this government cannot endure permanently half slave and half free. . . ." Several months later, Senator Seward echoed Lincoln's House Divided speech. The New York senator said the clash between the slave-owning South and the free-soil North was "an irrepressible conflict."

During the Lincoln-Douglas contest for senator, the two men debated each other seven times. At Freeport, Lincoln challenged Douglas to repeat and expand on his answer to the Dred Scott decision. Douglas did, and his response, the so-called Freeport Doctrine, cost him the support of many southern Democrats.

The Republicans made encouraging gains in the state election of November 2, 1858, but the Democrats held their majority in the legislature. On January 5, 1859, both houses of the legislature met and elected Douglas to the United States Senate. (In Lincoln's time, senators were not elected by a direct vote of the people, so Lincoln and Douglas had been campaigning to elect members of the legislature who would vote for them.) Lincoln had lost his bid for a Senate seat, but he had won a national reputation. The drive to gain him the Republican Presidential nomination in 1860 began to pick up speed. As for Douglas, he went back to the Senate in Washington to find that the Democratic party was controlled by his southern enemies.

Senator Stephen A. Douglas used all his oratorical powers to keep the slavery issue from splitting the Democratic party. But during the Lincoln-Douglas debates, Lincoln needled the Little Giant into saying that the Dred Scott decision could not aid slave owners if a territorial legislature refused to pass laws protecting slavery. This statement turned thousands of southerners against Douglas and did much to bring a split in the party that cost Douglas the Presidency in 1860.

On December 2, 1859, John Brown was hanged in Charlestown, Virginia, after his capture while leading a raid on Harpers Ferry. His expedition convinced many southerners that the North wanted to loose murder and pillage on them. But only a few of the most violent abolitionists supported Brown. (Frank Leslie's Illustrated Newspaper)

Lincoln is Nominated for President

The country seemed calmer in the autumn of 1859. Then fanatical John Brown, who had murdered several men during the fighting in Kansas, sent a shock wave of anger and fear through the South. With a handful of followers, Brown seized the federal arsenal and armory at Harpers Ferry, Virginia. Slaves in the area did not rise against their masters, as Brown had hoped, and he was soon captured. Brown and six of his men were tried, convicted, and hanged at Charlestown, Virginia. Before he died, Brown wrote a warning to the nation: "I, John Brown, am now quite certain that the crimes of this guilty land will never be purged away but with blood. I had, as I now think, vainly flattered myself that without much bloodshed it might be done." Within two years, Union troops would march into battle singing "John Brown's Body."

Many southerners remembered Nat Turner's bloody revolt. Now, John Brown's crazy expedition convinced them that the North wanted to loose murder and pillage upon them. But only a few violent abolitionists backed Brown, and Republican leaders were quick to deplore the raid. Lincoln said that "No man, North or South, can approve of violence or crime."

Douglas attacked Lincoln and Seward, saying that the House Divided and Irrepressible Conflict speeches had helped trigger Brown's raid. But Douglas himself soon was under attack from southern Democrats. Led by Senator Jefferson Davis of Mississippi, they demanded that the federal government protect slavery in all territories. They charged that Douglas' Freeport Doctrine answer to the Dred Scott decision was actually an attack on slavery. Grimly, Douglas warned southern Democrats that the party could not hope to win the Presidency with a program that would have the United States government force the people of a territory to have slavery when they were opposed to it.

While Douglas was fighting for his political life, Lincoln's political fortunes were steadily improving. At Cooper Union Institute in New York on February 27, 1860, he made one of his great speeches — a speech that did much to win him the Republican nomination for President. In this speech, Lincoln put the preservation of the Union ahead of any all-out attack on slavery. He spoke for those Republicans who agreed that slavery must be let alone in the South, but must not be allowed to spread into the territories. Lincoln agreed that it was difficult to convince southerners that the Republicans did not want to abolish slavery. "What will satisfy them?" he asked. "Simply this; we must not only let them alone, but we must somehow convince them that we do let them alone. This, we know from experience, is no easy task."

When the Democratic party met in Charleston, South Carolina, on April 23, 1860, to nominate a Presidential candidate, the Dred Scott decision was there like an unwelcome guest. Southern fire-eaters insisted that the Supreme Court's ruling had opened all territories to slavery and that the federal government must protect it. This bald demand for a slave code outraged supporters of Senator Douglas. They insisted that the settlers in a territory must be free to accept or reject slavery.

A majority of the delegates at Charleston favored Douglas, but they lacked the two-thirds majority needed to nominate him. The southern secessionists were determined to block his nomination. They would not accept Douglas' Freeport Doctrine. Douglas' opposition to the Lecompton constitution had also turned the supporters of President Buchanan against him. The Buchanan Democrats knew that Douglas was the party's strongest candidate. They feared that the dumping of Douglas would split the party and assure the election of a Republican. This was exactly what the secessionists were working for. They believed that the election of a "Black Republican" was just the jolt needed to drive all the southern states out of the Union. With this accomplished, an independent South could protect slavery from the wild men of the North.

When the secessionists' demand for a slave code in the territories was rejected by a majority of the convention, delegates of the southern cotton states walked out. A few days later, the rest of the disheartened delegates left Charleston. In Baltimore, on June 23, the northern Democrats nominated Douglas. Their platform pledged the party to obey the Dred Scott decision regarding the rights of property in the territories. A week later, southern Democrats met in Richmond, Virginia, and designated as their Presidential candidate Buchanan's Vice-President, John C. Breckinridge of Kentucky. They flatly demanded that all territories be opened to slavery and that Cuba be annexed by the United States. The Democratic party was hopelessly split. Observing the ruins of his party, Alexander Stephens of Georgia sadly said: "Men will be cutting one another's throats in a little while. In less than 12 months, we shall be in a war, and that the bloodiest in history."

When the Republicans met in Chicago on May 16, they were in high spirits because of the split in the Democratic party. Lincoln's managers worked hard to win delegate support away from Senator Seward of New York, and on the third ballot, the Illinois lawyer was nominated. Clearly he was not the first choice of many delegates, but he had fewer enemies than the other contenders. The Republican platform opposed the Dred Scott decision and declared that neither Congress nor a territorial legislature could legalize slavery in the territories.

Earlier, on May 8, a collection of conservative Whigs and Know-Nothings from twenty-two states met in Baltimore and organized the Constitutional Union party. A leading candidate for the Presidential nomination was Governor Sam Houston of Texas. After losing his Senate seat because of his pro-Union stand, Houston had won the governorship as an independent candidate. Correspondents of *The New York Times*, the *Herald*, and the *Tribune* all predicted his nomination. Houston's watchwords, "The Constitution and the Union," stirred many men who felt he could prevent disunion and war. But old-line Whigs distrusted the plain-speaking Houston. They worked for the loyal, veteran Whig from Tennessee, John Bell. He was nominated on the second ballot. The party platform merely called for: "The Constitution of the country, the Union of the States and the enforcement of the laws." Its failure even to mention slavery caused its foes to dub it the Do-Nothing party.

Secession Spreads—The Confederacy Is Formed

In the election of 1860, the three anti-Republican candidates polled nearly a million more popular votes than Lincoln. But Lincoln got 180 electoral votes to Breckinridge's 72, Bell's 39, and Douglas' 12. The man from Illinois would have won even if all anti-Republican votes had gone to one candidate. Bell and Douglas together polled 124,000 more votes than the secessionist candidate, Breckinridge. Despite the noise made by secessionists, there were thousands of southerners who believed in the Union. But they were not organized, while the secessionists were not only organized but knew exactly what they wanted to do. They were determined to organize a new nation.

Shortly after Lincoln's election, the South Carolina legislature called a convention to meet in December. An ordinance of secession was passed without debate on December 20, 1860. Explaining their action, the delegates complained that the North had "denounced as sinful the institution of slavery . . . [and] united in the election of a

[42]

CHARLESTON

MERCURY

EXTRA:

Passed unanimously at 1.15 o'clock, P. M., December 20th, 1860.

AN ORDINANCE

To dissolve the Union between the State of South Carolina and other States united with her under the compact entitled " The Constitution of the United States of America."

We, the People of the State of South Carolina, in Convention assembled, do declare and ordain, and it is hereby declared and ordained,

That the Ordinance adopted by us in Convention, on the twenty-third day of May, in the year of our Lord one thousand seven hundred and eighty-eight, whereby the Constitution of the United States of America was ratified, and also, all Acts and parts of Acts of the General Assembly of this State, ratifying amendments of the said Constitution, are hereby repealed; and that the union now subsisting between South Carolina and other States, under the name of "The United States of America," is hereby dissolved.

THE

UNION

IS

DISSOLVED!

Southern secessionists warned during the 1860 Presidential campaign that the election of a "Black Republican" would force the South to secede from the Union. Shortly after Lincoln's election, the South Carolina legislature called a convention to meet in December, and its fateful action is reported above. The hesitant, bumbling Buchanan told Congress that no state had the right to secede, but lamely added that the federal government had no power to act against a seceding state. (New York Public Library) man to the high office of President of the United States whose opinions and purposes are hostile to slavery."

Fire-eaters in other southern states now urged for secession. Alexander Stephens led the moderates who wanted the South to delay this step. They thought the South should wait and see what Lincoln did when he took office. They further pointed out that in the new Congress the Republicans would be outvoted 37 to 29 in the Senate and 129 to 108 in the House. Stephens talked common sense: "The President is no emperor, no dictator — he is clothed with no absolute power. He can do nothing unless he is backed by power in Congress. . . ."

Stephens and Lincoln had become friends when they were Whig congressmen in 1847-49. Lincoln read Stephens' speech and then wrote to the Georgian: "Do the people of the South really entertain fears that a Republican administration would directly, or indirectly interfere with the slaves, or with them about their slaves? If they do, I wish to assure you, as once a friend, and still, I hope, not an enemy, that there is no cause for such fears. . . . I suppose, however, that this does not meet the case. You think slavery is right and ought to be extended, while we think it is wrong and ought to be restricted. That, I suppose, is the rub. It certainly is the only substantial difference between us."

Southern secessionists were in no mood to heed Lincoln. During January and February of 1861, six cotton states — Florida, Alabama, Georgia, Mississippi, Louisiana, and Texas — joined South Carolina in seceding from the Union. Speaking of the secessionists, Stephens said: "They are run mad. . . . They are wild with passion and frenzy, doing they know not what."

In Washington, the hesitant, weak-kneed President Buchanan told Congress that no state had the right to secede from the Union. But he added that the federal government had no power to take action against a seceding state.

Virginia stayed in the Union a little longer, and its leaders organized a peace convention of northern and southern politicians, which met in Washington. But while these delegates sought ways to keep the Union together, other delegates from seven southern states met in Montgomery, Alabama. They established the Confederate States of America and elected Jefferson Davis provisional president. Alexander Stephens was named provisional vice-president. Both men had been moderates who had been urging a go-slow policy. But when the step was taken, they were loyal to the South.

In Texas, Governor Houston was forced from office when he refused to take the oath of allegiance to the Confederacy. While crowds celebrated, the stubborn old man wrote a farewell message: "Fellow citizens, in the name of your rights, which I believe have been trampled upon, I refuse to take this oath. In the name of my own conscience and my own manhood . . . I refuse to take this oath. . . ."

Back in Washington, Senator John C. Crittenden of Kentucky offered a compromise to bring the seceded states back into the Union. He proposed an amendment to the Constitution that would prevent Congress from ever abolishing slavery in the South. He also proposed that the Missouri Compromise line be extended west to the Pacific Coast. All territory north of the line would be forever free; all territory south of the line would be forever slave. Many prominent politicians and businessmen in the North supported the Crittenden compromise. Lincoln flatly turned down the plan to run the Missouri Compromise line to the Pacific. He had been elected on a pledge to keep slavery out of the territories, and he meant to honor that pledge. As he often put it, "We must give them [the territories] a clean bed with no snakes in it."

The compromisers argued that the West was not suited to slavery, and the whole issue was in reality nonexistent. They pointed out that there were only ten slaves in Nebraska and two in Kansas. Lincoln's supporters answered southerners in this manner: "You say the issue

[45]

is nonexistent because slavery cannot thrive in the West. But you still are willing to split the Union to defend the right to plant slavery in the West!" Lincoln himself believed that giving in to the slave owners would only whet their appetites for more later. He felt that their future demands might include the restoration of the slave trade and war in Cuba and Mexico in order to get more slave territory.

Clearly, the planters of the South were being squeezed hard by the rising cost of slaves and the high cost of borrowing money from northern bankers. Many of them were demanding the restoration of the slave trade. They also wanted measures adopted in Congress to prevent the organization of more free states in the territories. Slavery was the planters' way of life. If it could not be protected and expanded within the Union, the planters were ready to set up an independent nation. Perhaps the Crittenden compromise would have brought the southern states back into the Union. But would this compromise have worked any longer than the one that was tried in 1850? Unfortunately, history does not reveal what *might* have happened. Lincoln appears to have thought the problem over carefully when he wrote to Senator Lyman Trumbull of Illinois: "Let there be no compromise on the question of *extending* slavery. If there be, all our labor is lost, and ere long, must be done again. . . ." The President-elect's opposition killed the Crittenden compromise in Congress.

Aftermath of the Dred Scott Decision

In his inaugural address on March 4, 1861, Lincoln again emphasized that he had no intention of interfering with slavery in the South. He then argued strongly against the wisdom of secession: "Physically speaking, we cannot separate. We cannot remove our respective sections from each other, nor build an impassable wall between them. A husband and wife may be divorced, and go out of the presence and

[46]

The oath of office was administered by the frail, eighty-four-year-old Chief Justice Taney. Then, Lincoln read his inaugural address in which he bluntly warned the South: ". . . No state upon its own mere motion, can lawfully get out of the Union. . . . In your hands, my dissatisfied fellow countrymen, and not mine, is the momentous issue of civil war. . . ." (National Park Service)

beyond the reach of each other, but the different parts of our country cannot do this. They cannot but remain face to face; and intercourse, either amicable or hostile, must continue between them. Is it possible then, to make that intercourse more advantageous or more satisfactory *after* separation than *before*? Can aliens make treaties easier than friends can make laws? Can treaties be more faithfully enforced between aliens, than laws among friends? Suppose you go to war, you cannot fight always; and when, after much loss on both sides, and no gain on either, you cease fighting, the identical old questions, as to terms of intercourse, are again upon you. . . ."

Near the close of his address, Lincoln put the issue of peace or war squarely up to the South. "It is safe to assert that no government proper ever had provision in its organic law for its own termination. . . . No state upon its own mere motion, can lawfully get out of the Union. . . . In your hands, my dissatisfied fellow countrymen, and not mine, is the momentous issue of civil war. The government will not assail you. You can have no conflict, without being yourselves the aggressors. You have no oath registered in Heaven to destroy the government, while I shall have the most solemn one to 'preserve, protect and defend' it. . . ."

Here was no James Buchanan, telling the states they could not secede from the Union and then saying — almost in the same breath — the government had no power to act against seceding states. Buchanan, who trustingly felt that a Supreme Court decision could "settle" the emotion-charged slavery question, still felt that the Presidency had no power to "preserve, protect and defend" the Union. Buchanan drew no inspiration, no strength, from the example of President Andrew Jackson when he forced South Carolina to obey the laws of the land in 1833.

After the Confederate attack on Fort Sumter in April of 1861 had brought Civil War, Lincoln told a special session of Congress: "This issue embraces more than the fate of these United States. It presents to

[48]

THE LATEST NEWS.

TELEGRAPHIC.

NOTICE.—The *Star* is the only afternoon paper published in Washington city that receives the dispatches of the Associated Press.

THE WAR COMMENCED.

CONFLICT AT CHARLESTON.

IMMENSE EXCITEMENT.

Bombardment of Fort Sumter.

The Fire Returned by Maj. Anderson.

Correspondence between Gen Beauregard and Major Anderson.

TWO GUNS AT FORT SUMTER SILENCED.

BREACH IN THE FORT REPORTED.

Arrival of U. S. Ships of War off the Bar.

CHARLESTON, April 12.—The excitement prevailing here for several days past rose to the very highest pitch this morning, when it was ascertained that war had been actually commenced and Fort Sumter attacked by the forces of South Carolina.

It appears the fire was opened on Sumter about four o'clock this morning with considerable spirit from the batteries on Sullivan's Island, (where Fort Moultrie is situate,) Cummings' Point, Morris Island, and other points.

Major Anderson returned the fire, and a brisk

This dispatch from Charleston, South Carolina, appearing in the Washington Evening Star, *April 13, 1861, reported the opening shots of the Civil War. On April 15, Lincoln called for seventy-five thousand volunteers and later told a special session of Congress that "No choice was left but to call out the war power of the Government . . . for its preservation." (Washington* Evening Star)

the whole family of man, the question, whether a constitutional republic, or a democracy — a government of the people, by the same people — can, or cannot, maintain its territorial integrity, against its own domestic foes. . . . It forces us to ask: Is there, in all republics, this inherent, and fatal weakness? Must a government, of necessity, be too *strong* for the liberties of its own people, or too *weak* to maintain its own existence?

"So viewing the issue, no choice was left but to call out the war power of the Government; and so to resist force, employed for its destruction, by force, for its preservation."

During the cruel war years, Lincoln continued to clash with

[49]

Chief Justice Taney. The sickly, bitter Taney, still certain he had been right all along, was ready to pounce on any government action that he considered illegal. To combat the activities of persons who opposed the war, Lincoln had suspended the writ of habeas corpus.* This meant that a person could be arrested and imprisoned without a trial in the regular civil courts. In a test case of this, John Merryman, a strong secessionist, was arrested and brought to Fort McHenry in Baltimore, Maryland. Taney, who was sitting as a circuit judge at the time, issued a writ of habeas corpus, which directed General Cadwalader, the military commander at Fort McHenry, to bring Merryman to the Baltimore federal court. Cadwalader refused to obey because Lincoln had suspended the right to habeas corpus. Taney then sent a United States marshal to arrest the general for contempt of court. The marshal was brusquely turned away by a sentry, and Taney did not send him back, but instead wrote an opinion, known as *Ex parte Merryman*. In it, he declared that Congress alone, not the President, had the power to suspend the right to habeas corpus. When Taney sent his opinion to Lincoln, the President turned it over to his Attorney General. That official told Lincoln that Taney was wrong, so the President simply ignored *Ex parte Merryman*. The Supreme Court's blunder in the Dred Scott case had so weakened its standing with the public that few complaints were voiced when Lincoln shrugged off Taney's opinion.

For the next three years, Taney continued to oppose practically any and all government actions. The steady growth of Lincoln's war powers set Taney's teeth on edge. When the Supreme Court decided by a 5 to 4 vote that Lincoln had the power to blockade the southern

---

* *Habeas corpus*, a Latin expression for "you have the body." It is a legal writ directing a person detaining another to produce the party before a court or judge for inquiry into the cause of detention. It is basically used to test the validity of imprisonment and to release the prisoner in the event that the imprisonment is invalid.

coast, Taney was one of the dissenters. He also wrote other opinions on cases that had not reached the Court. Taney wanted to be ready if given a chance. One opinion held that the conscription act — drafting men for war service — was unconstitutional. Another Taney opinion ruled against Lincoln's Emancipation Proclamation, freeing the slaves in the Confederacy.

In 1864, at the age of eighty-seven, the combative Chief Justice died. At a memorial service of the Boston bar, a generous tribute to his long career was delivered by ex-Justice Benjamin R. Curtis, who had clashed so bitterly with him in 1857.

After the war ended, Congress in 1868 passed the Fourteenth Amendment to the Constitution, and ratification of it by the states was completed on July 28 of that year. This amendment set aside the Dred Scott decision by declaring Negroes, and all others born or naturalized in the United States, citizens of the United States.

Dred Scott himself did not live to hear this news. He died in St. Louis in 1858 — ten years before the ratification of the amendment that would have made him a United States citizen.

BIBLIOGRAPHY

Hofstadter, Richard. *The American Political Tradition*. New York: Random House (Vintage Books), 1948.

Swisher, Carl B. *Roger B. Taney*. New York: Macmillan, 1936.

Warren, Charles. *The Supreme Court in United States History*, vol. 2, revised edition. Boston: Little, Brown, 1960.

Pfeffer, Leo. *This Honorable Court*. Boston: Beacon Press, 1965.

Agar, Herbert. *The Price of Union*. Boston: Houghton Mifflin Company, 1950.

Basler, Roy P. *Abraham Lincoln, His Speeches and Writings*. Cleveland, Ohio: World, 1946.

Franklin, John Hope. *From Slavery to Freedom, A History of Negro Americans*, 3rd edition. New York: Alfred A. Knopf, 1967.

Index